A gift of love to the
OCF Students
from the parish of
† St. Andrew

2016

The Spiritual
Archimandrite ... siev

A priest, after hearing the confession, places his epitrachelion over the head of the penitent and says the following prayer:

May our Lord and God, Jesus Christ, through the grace and lovingkindness of His love for mankind, forgive thee, O child, all thy sins; and I, an unworthy priest, through His power given to me, forgive and release thee of all thy sins, in the name of the Father, and the Son, and the Holy Spirit. Amen.

The Forgotten Medicine

THE MYSTERY OF REPENTANCE

By Archimandrite Seraphim Aleksiev
Translated by Ralitsa Doynova

2006

Second Printing 1995
Third Printing 1998
Fourth Printing 2001
Fifth Printing 2003
Second Edition, Sixth Printing 2006

Address all correspondence to:
St. Xenia Skete
P.O. Box 260, Wildwood, California 96076

Front Cover: "An angel crowns the Sacrament of Penance while the devil flees." A 19th-century engraving from the book, *Spiritual Instructions to the Penitent,* published by the Russian St. Panteleimon Monastery of Mt. Athos, Moscow, 1901.

Library of Congress Cataloging in Publication Data
Seraphim Aleksiev, Archimandrite
The forgotten medicine: the mystery of repentance.
Translated from the Bulgarian.

Library of Congress Catalogue Number: 94-66581
ISBN 0-938635-49-4

CONTENTS

Archimandrite Seraphim (Aleksiev)

About the Author

ARCHIMANDRITE SERAPHIM Aleksiev was born in 1912 in Bulgaria. He acquired his education in the Theological Seminary in Sophia, and afterwards went to study in Switzerland. In 1940 he took monastic vows. His acquaintance with Archbishop Seraphim Sobolev (†1950)[1] played a decisive role in his life. In the person of the Archbishop, Archimandrite Seraphim found an irreplaceable guide in the Faith and in his spiritual life.

Three periods can be defined in the life and creative work of Father Seraphim. During the first (1947-1960), he, as the director of the Cultural and Educational Department of the Holy Synod and despite the difficult conditions of the time, maintained tireless pastoral activity, delivered inspired sermons and lectures, and wrote brochures and books on spiritual and moral themes, and many poems. The collections of lectures *Our Hope* and *Our Love,* two of his most popular books, are very characteristic of this period. During the second period (1960-1969), Archimandrite Seraphim—already an assistant

1. Editor's Note: Archbishop Seraphim Sobolev not only was an outstanding theologian defending Patristic Orthodoxy, but was also a miracle-worker. He had a close relationship, through prayer, with St. Seraphim of Sarov, with whose blessing he embraced monasticism. His concern for Orthodox dogmatic purity and precision moved him to write a treatise against a false interpretation of the dogma of Redemption, and also a lengthy work against the erroneous teaching of "sophiology."

professor in Dogmatic Theology in the Theological Academy in Sophia—published a series of theological studies. The third period began in 1969, when he was forced to leave the Theological Academy because of a disagreement in principle with the calendar reform, which was adopted then, and with the pro-ecumenical policy with which the Bulgarian Orthodox Church had become involved. Outside the Academy, Archimandrite Seraphim wrote a new series of books with a theological, spiritual, and moral content, among which was his last book and legacy: *Orthodoxy and Ecumenism* (1992)—an in-depth criticism of the ecumenical heresy.

Archimandrite Seraphim reposed on January 13/26, 1993. He left us a precious inheritance: his books and his example of a zealous monastic life wholly dedicated to the service of the holy Orthodox Faith.

A Note of Introduction

Blessed are the pure in heart: for they shall see God.
Matthew 5:8

IN READING these words, every Christian feels a natural yearning of the heart towards God, a true desire to taste the sweetness of communion, of being with Him as He created us to be; but the impurity of our hearts—full of passions, conflicts, and fears—bars the way. Yet, there is a cure for the weight of sin which burdens the heart and soul of each one of us and afflicts the conscience, keeping us from inner peace and from peace with our neighbors and loved ones.

"In the Mystery of Repentance the spiritual afflictions of a man are treated, impurities of soul are removed, and a Christian, having received forgiveness of sins, again becomes innocent and sanctified, just as he came out of the waters of Baptism."[1] St. Theophan the Recluse tells us that "in the Sacrament ... of Confession the Lord enters into man by His grace, vividly establishes communion with him, and gives him to taste of all the sweetness of the Divine...."[2]

If such blessed transformation and heavenly consolation come through the Mystery of Repentance, why do we not hasten

1. Protopresbyter Michael Pomazansky, *Orthodox Dogmatic Theology* (Platina, California: St. Herman of Alaska Brotherhood, 1984), p. 287.
2. Quoted by Igumen Chariton of Valamo, *The Art of Prayer* (London: Faber and Faber, 1985), p. 171.

to partake of it? Archimandrite Seraphim in *The Forgotten Medicine* details the reasons many have for not coming to Confession, and for each of these he clearly brings forth the truth of the matter. For those who feel awkward because of not knowing how to approach Confession, he explains in depth how to prepare before, what to do when we are with the confessor, and what to do afterwards. He then writes of the wondrous changes in the lives of those who enter into the Mystery of Repentance, illustrating with several true accounts.

As we read the words of Archimandrite Seraphim, let us take to heart his counsel, so that we may also know in truth the words of the Psalmist, *Blessed are they whose iniquities are forgiven and whose sins are covered* (Psalm 31:1).

St. Xenia Skete
Great Lent, 1994

I

The Rich Traveller

INTO A REMOTE and beautiful mountain village came an unusual stranger for his summer vacation. He was a very rich man. He was travelling alone, and, being quite tired, he wanted to find a place to stay and rest. He had the intention of rewarding the people who could give him a quiet and pleasant stay. Since he had countless riches, he wanted to give his cordial hosts a present that they had never even dreamed of.

He saw what seemed to be a beautiful house situated on a wonderful spot and decided to ask for shelter there. He knocked on the door, but when it was opened and he was invited to come in, he instinctively shrank away. An unbearably foul-smelling air reached him from inside. What was the matter? The home of these people and their pigsty were under the same roof. Without even mentioning the reason for his visit, the traveller excused himself and went back out into the yard.

He went along the clear river which was running through the village. Close by was another beautiful, newly built house which attracted his attention, and he decided to knock at its door. However, the owner of this home was a very cruel man. When he saw a stranger approaching the gates, he set his dogs on him and did not even let him come into his yard.

The traveller sought shelter in a third house as well. The people there invited him kindly, and he went inside. But after he saw that everything in this home was lying around in disorder, covered with dust and soot, and buried in waste and cobwebs, he decided that he would not be able to find the longed-for peace.

By that time, he was so tired that he decided to stay in the next, fourth house no matter what its condition. But there, besides the untidiness and the dirt, he noticed something else. There were signs of bedbugs on the walls, and he could not stand the parasites. Also, fleas crawled all over him, so he hurried to get out of there, too.

In this way he went about the whole village, but he could not find a clean home where he could rest peacefully. He wondered how these people, who lived in such a beautiful mountain country, could abandon their houses so. A small river ran through the village. Creeks spouted out from many places in the steep and curvy streets. In the square and in other places in the village there were spouts and fountains from which abundant water gushed out. It was clear to the traveller that the filth in the village houses was due not to the lack of water, but exclusively to the negligence of the owners.

At the end of the village, exhausted, he dropped by a small house in which, as it turned out, lived a good housewife. There he was met with great cordiality and with friendly, smiling faces. The moment he entered one of the rooms, he noticed that everything there was simple, but clean and well ordered. The windows were shining with cleanliness. There were no cobwebs in the corners. The boards of the floor were recently cleaned. The air in the room was fresh. It was evident that the fragrance of the near fields and forests was often allowed to come into this house through the open windows.

The traveller sighed with relief and stayed in this home. At last he had found a quiet, pleasant place to rest. It was there that he left his magnificent gift.

Dear readers, have you asked yourselves: if our Saviour were to come, He Who is bringing the greatest gift—His heavenly grace with which He makes our souls happy and saves them—and if He were to seek a shelter for Himself in our souls, where could He find a place fit for rest? St. Macarius of Egypt says: "Just as God has created the heavens and the earth for man to inhabit, so He has created the body and the soul of man to be His abode, that is why the Apostle says, His *house we are*" (Heb. 3:6).[1]

Jesus Christ, this wondrous heavenly Guest, often comes among us and wishes to enter under the roof of our soul. He appears among us through the unfathomable mystery of Holy Communion. He knocks on every door, longs to come into every home, desires to talk with every heart, wants to make every believing soul happy and to give it His heavenly gift.

But how do we meet Him? Can He stay in each one of us as He would like to?

Here is a man approaching Holy Communion and inviting the Lord into the hidden room of his heart: "Come, Lord Jesus, and settle in me!" he whispers in his prayers before Communion. "Come under my roof, in the home of my soul; come in, please! I will open the doors of my heart! Settle in me!"

But Jesus Christ draws back with disgust from these hospitably opened doors! Such an unbearable spiritual stench is coming from the inside! There it stinks of debauchery and malice, of avarice and envy, of pride and selfishness.... And the heavenly Guest draws back. He cannot enter such a home, where

1. St. Macarius the Great, *Spiritual Discourses, Epistles, and Speeches,* 4th edition, (Holy Trinity- St. Sergius Lavra, 1904).

the man and the demons—these spiritual pigs—are co-existing under the same roof.

Here people are exhorting one to fast and take Communion. They are asking him to accept in his heart Jesus Christ Who is bringing the great and all-saving grace of God, the highest gift ever received by mankind, but he does not want to hear about it; the holy heavenly things are unpleasant to him!... They are preventing him from living any way he wants to. Why does he need Communion? He sets the dogs in his soul against the heavenly Guest and does not let Him approach his gates.

A third one has fasted, prayed, and prepared for Holy Communion, but he has not forgiven the offenses which his neighbors have committed against him, has not made peace with his enemies, has not pacified his soul. Everything in it is in disorder. The sins are covering his outward piety like dust and soot. Waste and cobwebs have marred his faith. Bad moods have confused his feelings. And in this condition he dares to invite the heavenly Guest into the room of his heart! Is he not afraid that he will offend Him instead of pleasing Him with this hospitality?

A fourth one hears that someone is knocking on the door of his conscience, but until now it has not occurred to him to clean it. There, so many vicious spots have dirtied the once-clean windows of the soul! So many sinful habits have piled waste in the secret corners of the heart! The poor man! The parasites of evil, the evil spirits, have attacked him and are drawing the life-juices of his spiritual life. If he opens the doors and invites the highest heavenly Guest into such a condition of filth and disorder, does he think that he will give Him pure and joyful rest?

But who could say of his spiritual home that it is in full order and that he can welcome the heavenly King?

We are all more or less unworthy of the Redeemer coming from heaven. But here, He is knocking on our doors (cf. Rev. 3:20). He Himself longs to come into us, because we are created for Him and without Him we are infinitely unhappy. He is coming to bring His heavenly gift to everyone.

Is there a way for us to become worthy of Him again? With great joy we must say: There is! This way is Confession! Through Confession, when it is sincere, deep, and involves disgust with oneself and a desire to start a new life, the room of the heart is thoroughly cleaned from all the waste of the sins. Through Confession, the demons, these deadly parasites in the heart, are chased away. Through Confession, the windows of the soul are opened for the fragrance and the freshness of God's grace to come through them. Through Confession, all confused thoughts and ideas, all chaotic feelings and desires of the heart are once again put in order. At last, through Confession the soul is adorned, so that it becomes fit to accept the most marvelous guest—Jesus Christ.

A guardian angel indicates the way, saying, "Go, confess your sins to your spiritual father." The demon, however, opposing him, says, "You're still young, and whatever you have sinned as a young man you can confess on your deathbed."

A 19th-century engraving from the book, *Spiritual Instructions to the Penitent.*

II

Sin

DEAR READERS, we are created for God, and only in Him do we find the paramount bliss for which our heart is constantly yearning. Nothing other than God can make our souls happy! Give man everything which he desires. He will enjoy it for a while, but afterwards he will become indifferent to it, because he feels that something else, much more elevated, is missing. Is it not in that way that the child, too, enjoys every new toy until it grows hungry? Then it abandons the toy and looks for food. A certain inextinguishable inner hunger for truth, joy, and peace in the Holy Spirit (cf. Rom. 14:17) torments our soul and does not give us peace, even among the best pleasures of life and among the most enviable achievements in the world.

This blessed hunger is a hunger for God. Blessed Augustine is right in his *Confessions* before God: "Thou madest us for Thyself, and our heart is restless until it repose in Thee."[1]

The only guest who can make our soul happy is God. And if God is our paramount bliss, it is clear that that which obstructs the way to God must be the greatest evil for us. Such an evil is sin.

---

1. Dr. M. Stoyanov, *The Blessed Augustine's Road to God,* (Plovdiv, 1935), p. 3.

It is in vain that some unenlightened people seek the greatest evil for man somewhere else, rather than in sin. Some consider disease to be the greatest evil, others—poverty, and others—death. But neither disease, nor poverty, nor death, nor any other earthly disaster can be such a great evil for us as sin is. These earthly misfortunes do not separate us from God if we are seeking Him sincerely, but, on the contrary, they bring us closer to Him.

The holy Apostles were themselves poor but enriched many (cf. II Cor. 6:10). They were rich despite their poverty, because they possessed the marvelous gift of God—the heavenly grace which even in this life made them infinitely blissful! Is it possible that poverty could have been a great evil for them who had found the treasure of eternal life?

Disease is not the greatest evil for man, because a disease of the body endured with humility, faith, and patience can cure the soul sick with sin and bring it closer to God—the greatest good for man.

And death is not frightening for the believer, because through it, as through a door, one goes to the beloved and loving God Who hath prepared for them that love Him that which eye hath not seen, nor ear heard, neither have entered into the heart of man (cf. I Cor 2:9).

But sin is the most wretched poverty of the heart—poverty blocking the treasure of grace. Sin is a deadly sickness of the soul, a sickness which deprives us both of the joys of earth and the joys of heaven. Sin is a terrible and most lamentable spiritual death which separates us eternally from the joy of the heavenly inhabitants in paradise and buries us in the darkness of hell.

There is no greater evil for man than sin. It destroys both the body and the soul. It makes both this life and eternal life bitter. It causes discord in families, quarrels among neighbors, and disagreements among relatives. It starts the fire of malice among people. It makes the soul proud and embittered. It poisons the heart with envy. It drives out holy feelings from the breast and invites the demons to settle there. It separates us from God. It extinguishes everything bright in our hearts. It teaches us to lie, to be gluttonous, and to be selfish and greedy. It makes us slander and judge our neighbors. It incites our hand to steal. It fills us with anger and rage. It whispers to us to seek revenge. It commits all outrages, debaucheries, and crimes. It causes all diseases, suffering, injustice, violence, bloodshed, and war. It has filled the souls of all of us with unbearable spiritual stench. It pours this stench into the relationships among us.

Have you asked yourself why is it so stifling in the world? Why is it hard to live? Why can we not put up with each other? The answer is: because sin has poisoned the atmosphere of life. We are all sick with sin. And if untreated body wounds emit intolerable stench, how much more terrible is the stench of sin!

Just as the diseases of the body can be external (visible) and internal (hidden), so the sins, as diseases of the soul, can be visible and invisible. We often comfort ourselves with the fact that we can hide the sinful wounds of our soul from the eyes of those around us. We pass for good and respectable people in their eyes. But we cannot hide anything from God. His eyes are brighter than the sun and penetrate everywhere. If we could take pictures of, or, with the help of some spiritual x-rays, see the hidden spiritual condition of each of us or of the whole of mankind as God sees it, we would be terrified!

Sin is an infinite evil because it is an insult to the infinite God. The Lord has commanded us not to sin. But we sin, and thus we insult the infinite greatness of the Creator.

The Word of God says: *Sin is the transgression of the law* (I John 3:4). This means that sin is a violation of God's law. Every violated law, be it civil or natural, entails punishment. Sin, as a transgression of the highest law—the will of God, leads to most heavy punishments. These punishments can be temporary or eternal. The temporary ones are sent by God to bring us to our senses and for correction. If we repent and are reconciled with God, we will save ourselves from the eternal punishments. But if we remain with bitterness in our sins, if we do not want to repent of them, if we persist in our rebellion against God, He will let us go our own way.

The end result of sin is an ultimate separation from God. And since God is the happiness of the human heart, separation from God is the deprivation of that happiness, or eternal sorrow. If sin is such a terrible evil, why do all of us commit sin so carelessly? How have we gotten to the point of befriending our sins most intimately, of getting used to them to such a degree that most of us today think that sin is unavoidable in life? How have we been able to stand, and still stand, the filth, dust, and cobwebs in the rooms of our hearts, living with a dull insensibility in this disorder, amid the stench of our lawlessness?! All this is simply inexplicable. But it is a fact. Hardened, morally dulled, we have become indifferent towards the call of our own conscience and towards the concern for our salvation.... And this indifference has come to the point where we underestimate the weight and the fatefulness of our wickedness. We think that we are not doing anything really bad when we sin. Oh, if we could measure the whole weight of our sins and if we would feel clearly that this weight is pulling us towards the bottom of hell, we would rather agree that the earth swallow us and that the rocks bury us than for us to sin and anger God!

If we picture a pair of scales and put human sins on one of the dishes and on the other—the holiness of all the bright spirits of heaven and of all the righteous people who have lived on earth, then all the holiness in heaven and earth would not be able to lift up the dish of human sinfulness. Only the power of God can lift it up. That is why God sent to earth His Only Begotten Son Who was to atone for human sin with His sacrifice on Golgotha. Since then, all the sins of man from all times can be forgiven if repentance for them is offered. Since then, there is no sin which weighs more than the weight of God's mercy. *For God so loved the world, that He gave His only begotten Son, that whosoever believeth in Him should not perish, but have everlasting life* (John 3:16). *Behold the Lamb of God which taketh away the sin of the world* (John 1:29).

Take courage, sinners! There is deliverance for us! Jesus Christ, Who carried on His shoulders the sin of all humanity and Who paid our debts to God with His death on the cross, can take our sin on His shoulders as well. Is it not because of this that St. Andrew of Crete prays in the name of all of us who sin before God: "Take my heavy sinful burden away from me and give me tears of repentance!" We must shed **tears of repentance**, because there are only two kinds of water which can wash away the filth of sin: the water of baptism and the tears of repentance. Furthermore, as St. John Climacus asserts: "Greater than baptism itself is the fountain of tears after baptism, even though it is somewhat audacious to say so. For baptism is the washing away of evils that were in us before, but sins committed after baptism are washed away by tears. As baptism is received in infancy, we have all defiled it, but we cleanse it anew with tears. And if God in His love for mankind had not given us tears, those being saved would be few indeed and hard to find."[2]

---

2. St. John Climacus, *The Ladder of Divine Ascent,* (Boston, Massachusetts: Holy Transfiguration Monastery, 1978), Step 7:6, p. 71.

The act of Confession is performed in the invisible presence of an angel with Jesus Christ mercifully looking from the Cross. A 19th-century engraving.

III

The Forgotten Medicine

THE HOLY SACRAMENT of Confession can rightly be called "the Forgotten Medicine." The whole world is lying in evil. Every one of us is infected with the deadly disease of sin, and one can be cured from this disease! The medicine is provided, and it is miraculous at that. You are healed the moment you take it. But we do not reach for it, to be healed and to lighten our conscience. Why? Because we have forgotten and neglected it.

Why will ye die, O house of Israel? cries with sorrow the holy prophet Ezekiel. "Why will you die in your sins, Christians?" our Redeemer Jesus Christ calls to us with even greater sorrow. "Is there not deliverance from death for you? Why should you gladden the enemy of your salvation—satan? Did I not establish all-powerful repentance in My Church?" *I desire not the death of the ungodly, but that the ungodly should turn from his way and live: turn ye heartily from your way* (Ezek. 33:11). Repentance, this infinitely good gift, is given to you "at any time of life, and it works with the same power for any sin: it cleanses every sin, saves everyone who turns to God, be it even in the last minutes before death."[1]

1. St. Ignatius Brianchaninov, *Works*, Vol. 1 (St. Petersburg, 1905), p. 100.

There are earthly medicines for earthly diseases. And there is an Omnipotent Heavenly Doctor and heavenly medicines for the most terrible disease called sin. This Doctor is Jesus Christ. Because every sin is a transgression of God's holy law, only God can forgive sins with His wondrous omnipotence. He can blot out sins as if they had never existed. *Though your sins be as purple, I will make them white as snow; though they be as scarlet, I will make them white as wool* (Is. 1:18), He promises. But for this to happen, there is one requirement for us—**to repent truly.**

"Nobody is as gracious and merciful," says St. Mark the Ascetic, "as the Lord is, but even He does not forgive the sins of the man who does not repent; ... we are being condemned not because of the multitude of our evils, but because we do not want to repent."[2]

The omnipotence of the Lord can forgive human sins. Look how unfathomable is God's mercy! God has given His power of forgiving the sins of men to the Apostles and their successors in the persons of the bishops and priests. Why has God done so? To make repentance, and therefore the forgiveness of sin, even closer, more accessible, and more certain. *Receive ye the Holy Spirit,* said Jesus Christ to His holy Apostles. *Whose soever sins ye remit, they are remitted unto them; and whose soever sins ye retain, they are retained* (John 20:22-23). *Whatsoever ye shall bind on earth shall be bound in heaven: and whatsoever ye shall loose on earth shall be loosed in heaven* (Matt. 18:18).

How does the forgiving of sins occur?—**through the Sacrament of Confession.** The Christian burdened with sins goes to the priest with deep repentance in his soul and with a sincere desire to change and reveals to him in a detailed, frank, and full confession the secrets of his heart and conscience. The

2. *Dobrotolubie* (Philokalia), Vol. 1 (St. Petersburg, 1877), p. 479.

priest, convinced of the sincere repentance of the Christian and after the suitable introductory prayers, reads to him the sacramental prayer: "May our Lord and God Jesus Christ, according to the grace and kindness of His love for man, forgive you, child [name], all your transgressions; and I, the unworthy priest, through the power given to me by Him, forgive you and free you of all your sins, in the name of the Father, and the Son, and the Holy Spirit. Amen."

In that moment, whatever the priest is forgiving on earth is also being forgiven in heaven! Is there a greater mercy than this? We could not have believed that this is possible, if it had not been told us by the One Who never spoke an empty word or a lie (cf. I Peter 2:22).

Sin is a great evil with immeasurably heavy consequences—eternal torments in hell! But its cure, established by Jesus Christ, turns out to be so easy! This is simply incredible—just as Jesus Christ told the ten lepers: *Go shew yourselves unto the priests* (Luke 17:14), and they, when they went, were healed, so it is as if He were speaking to us, sinners: "You are sick with spiritual leprosy?! Do not be afraid! You will be healed. Just do this: go show yourselves to the priests."

If we ignore such a mercy of God, how many more punishments we will deserve, because we have not done for our salvation even that small thing which is given to us to do and which is so easy.

The Holy Bible tells us that the commander of the Syrian army, Naaman, was suffering from leprosy. When he heard that in the land of Israel there was a certain prophet of God—Elisha—who could heal him, he went with many servants and gifts to him and stopped before his gates. The holy prophet did not come out to meet him but sent people to tell him: *Go and wash seven times in Jordan, and thy flesh shall return to thee, and thou shalt be cleansed (IV Kings 5:10). Naaman got angry when he heard these words and said: I said within myself, he will surely come out to me and stand and call on the name of the Lord his God and lay his hand upon the place and recover the leper.* But he sends me to wash in the Jordan! *Are not the rivers of Damascus better than all the waters of Israel?.. And he turned and went away in a rage. And his servants came near and said to him, Suppose the prophet had spoken a great thing to thee, wouldst thou not perform it? Yet he has but said to thee, Wash and be cleansed* (IV Kings 5:11-13).

Naaman took the advice of his servants, immersed himself in the Jordan seven times, and his body was cleansed and renewed, so that it became like the body of a small child.

What a terrible disease is leprosy, and how easily the prophet of God cured it! Is it not through the same simple way that the curing of the most terrible disease—sin—occurs? Immerse yourself in the waves of deep repentance, and the grace of God will cleanse you from every sin. You will come out of the spiritual bath of the holy Sacrament of Confession with a renewed and clean soul, as the soul of a child.

It was sin that took down from heaven the first angel, the Morning Star. It was sin that drove Adam and Eve out of Paradise. It was sin that caused the flood of the world. This sin is also threatening to separate us forever from God and to send us eternally into the abysses of hell.

Even if God were to require that we give all our possessions to the poor, if He were to require from us that we fast all our lives or give up once and for all all earthly joys and comforts in order to atone for our sins and save ourselves from their ominous consequences, we should agree to anything, only to save ourselves from eternal torment in hell, to which our sin is dragging us. But look what a simple salvation God has established for us:

Go shew yourselves to the priests (Luke 17:14). Confess your sins before them. Repent with all your heart, and you will free yourselves from the chains of evil.

What reasonable man would ignore Confession after all this? We can save our souls only in two ways: either by not sinning at all, or by repenting from our sins. Since among men there are no sinless ones, if we want to be reconciled with God Whom we anger with daily transgressions of His holy will, there is only this one thing left for us to do: to repent sincerely and openly. Otherwise, we will not see the face of God, because nothing impure will enter the radiant heavenly city.

The prayer before Confession:

Here, O child, here Christ is present invisibly, accepting your confession. Do not be horrified, neither be afraid; conceal nothing from me and without hesitation say all that you have done so that you will receive remission from Jesus Christ our Lord.

IV

Objections to Confession

HOW GREAT must be our wickedness! We do not turn to Confession not only because we forget about it, but we do not practice it even when we know about it. What can be more imprudent than this?

Confession is so important to us sinners that we must boldly say: there is no salvation for us without Confession. Abba Isaiah expresses the same thought: "If there were no repentance, nobody would be saved. Just as Baptism cleanses us from original sin and from all sins committed prior to Baptism, so repentance, involving a confession of our sins, cleanses us from all lawlessness committed after Baptism."

We do not confess because we have objections to Confession. What are our objections usually?

Here are the main ones:

1) One says: "I am so sinful! Can God forgive my sins? I do not believe this! That is why there is no use for me to go to Confession."

But if a man repents sincerely, any sin can be forgiven him. "The power of repentance is based on the power of God. The

Doctor is all-powerful, and the Medicine given by Him is all-powerful" (Bishop Ignatius Brianchaninov).

St. John Chrysostom, pondering on the miraculous results of sincere repentance, says: "Repentance is a medicine which destroys sin. It is a heavenly gift, a marvelous force which through the grace of God conquers the might and strictness of the laws. It accepts all and transforms all. It does not reject the fornicator, does not send away the adulterer, is not disgusted with the drunkard, does not loathe the idolater, does not neglect the slanderer, does not persecute the reviler nor the haughty man: it regenerates everybody because it is a furnace for purification from sin. The wound and the medicine, these are sin and Repentance" [Confession—author's note].

Do not tell me: "I have sinned much, how can I save myself?" You cannot, but your God can, and He can do it so that all your sins will be destroyed. Listen carefully to my words: your God destroys your sins in such a manner that there is neither a spot nor trace left of them, and as He restores your health, He presents you with the righteousness which frees you from the death penalty. He gives you righteousness; and the one who has sinned He makes equal to the one who has not, because He destroys sin and makes it disappear as if it had never been.

"But is it possible," you will say, "for the one who repents to be saved?" It is perfectly possible! "But I have spent my entire life in sin: if I repent, will I be saved?" Of course! "How do we know that?" From the love of your God for man. Am I relying on your repentance to destroy your heavy sins? If you were to rely only on your repentance, then, indeed, you should tremble; but the mercy of God unites with repentance. And the mercy of God has no limits; words cannot express His kindness. Your wickedness has an end, but the Medicine for it is boundless! Your wickedness is human wickedness, but God's mercy is ineffable, so, have hope that it will exceed your sins. Imagine a spark which falls in the sea: will it start a fire? Will it appear again? Sin is to God's love for man what the spark is to the sea, not even that, but something much smaller! The sea, however big it may be, has an end, but God's love for man is limitless.

2) Another says: "Why should I go to Confession? I have no special sins. Let those who have murdered, stolen, raped, or committed some other sin go to Confession."

This objection to Confession is the complete opposite of the first one. There the man, because of the oppressing realization of his wickedness, does not believe that he can be forgiven. Here, there is a lack of any realization of wickedness. "I have no special sins...." But is it really so? When a man stays in a closed room for a long time, he gets used to the bad air in it and does not feel how unpleasant it is. But if someone comes in from outside, he will not be able to stand the stench in the room and will run away.

Let those who say, "I have no special sins," answer whether they have Christ in their hearts. He likes to inhabit pure hearts. But are their hearts pure? Hardly! They imagine that they are pure, but imagination is not reality. *If we say that we have no sin, we deceive ourselves, and the truth is not in us* (I John 1:8). And where there is a lie, there Christ is not.

Then, what should we do?—let us confess. *If we confess our sins, He is faithful and just ... to cleanse us from all unrighteousness* (I John 1:9).

The Holy Fathers teach us that it is very hard for a man to see his sins. They explain this with the blindness caused by the devil. Abba Isaiah says: "When a man separates from the one on his left side, i.e. from communion with the demons and from following their suggestions, then he will see his sins against God in full; then he will know Jesus. But a man cannot see his sins until he separates himself from them through a separation filled with labor and distress. Those who have reached this condition have found tears and prayers; as they remember about their sly friendship with the passions, they do not dare to look towards God, and live constantly with a broken spirit."

If it were easy to see our sins, St. Ephraim the Syrian would not have prayed: "Lord, enable me to see my transgressions." Neither would Father John of Kronstadt say: "This is truly a gift of God—to be able to see your sins in their multitude and in all their loathsomeness."

It turns out that those who think that they do not have any great sins are actually blind. They must pray to God to enable them to perceive their sins and to save themselves from the extremely fatal spiritual delusion that they do not have any particular sins. Even if their sins are as small as specks of dust, if they are not cleaned with constant Confession, they pile up and dirty the room of the heart so that the high heavenly Guest cannot enter there.

The small sins are often more dangerous than the greatest crimes, because the latter weigh heavily on the conscience and insist on being atoned for, confessed, settled, erased, while the small sins do not weigh too much on the soul, but they have that perilous property of making it insensitive to the grace of God and indifferent to salvation. Fewer people have perished from ferocious wild beasts than have from small microbes, invisible to the naked eye. By being considered insignificant, the small sins are usually passed by without any attention. They are easily forgotten, but they create in man the most terrible habit—the habit of sinning, of dulling his moral consciousness. Thus the wretched sinner comes to deceive himself that he is not sinful, that everything is all right with him, when he is both a miserable and abject slave of sin.

Small sins create a true stagnation in the spiritual life of man. Just as the wall clock stops because of the accumulation of fine dust, so the spiritual pulse of man gradually dies out under the thick layer of accumulated small sins. In order for the clock to start running again, the dust must be blown out. In order for man to restore his spiritual life, he needs to confess even the smallest of his sins.

3) A third man says: "All this is true. But why should I confess when I know that tomorrow I will sin again? Is there any point in such confession? I see that one should confess only if one would sin no more after that!"

This objection to Confession contains both something which is very true and something which is not. The right thing here is the desire not to sin any more after Confession. But we are feeble humans, and we cannot attain right away such a firmness which makes falling into voluntary sins impossible. If we cannot reach such steadfastness in virtue right away, should we surrender to vice? Or should we stop confessing? Which is better—to roll in the mud of the spiritual swamp, or to pick yourself up after each fall and go on with the hope that someday you may reach the solid and beautiful shore of virtue? If you do not confess, you remain in the mud. If you confess, you pick yourself up from the mud and clean yourself. "But why should I get up if tomorrow I will fall again?" you say. When you fall again, then get up again! Every day begin all over again! This is undoubtedly better than falling out of the habit of getting up.

A young monk complained to the great ascetic Abba Sisoes: "Abba, what should I do? I fell." The elder answered: "Get up!" The monk said: "I got up, and I fell again!" The elder replied:

"Get up again!" But the young monk asked: "For how long should I get up when I fall?" "Until your death," answered Abba Sisoes.

This wise dialogue should be remembered by all of us who want to change but, deceived by the devil, constantly return to our previous sins. Every time we fall into a transgression, we must get up. The "getting up"—this is **Confession.**

"But why should we play at falling and getting up?" ask some. It is not a game, but a struggle in which there is much sense. If we, as feeble humans, fall but get up again, there is a great probability that death will find us when we are standing. Then we are saved. But if we do not intend to get up, death will surely find us lying in the mud. Then we are lost forever!

St. John Chrysostom says: "Repentance opens the heavens for man, takes him to Paradise, overcomes the devil. Have you sinned? Do not despair! If you sin every day, then offer repentance every day! When there are rotten parts in old houses, we replace the parts with new ones, and we do not stop caring for the houses. In the same way, you should reason for yourself: if today you have defiled yourself with sin, immediately clean yourself with repentance."[1]

For the washing away of bodily dirtiness God has given water. And for the washing of spiritual foulness, God has given the grace of the holy Sacrament of Confession. Every man, when he dirties his hands, washes them. No one says: "I will not wash my hands any more, because I will get them dirty again!" But why is it then that many people say, "I will not go to Confession, because I will sin again tomorrow!" It is clear that the enemy of our salvation is enticing us not to wash our souls, so that he can gain power over them.

1. St. John Chrysostom, *Works*, Vol. 2, Book 3 (St. Petersburg, 1896), p. 377.

But we must not give in to such satanic suggestions; we should confess frequently, because frequent washing produces a taste for cleanliness in us.

Leave your house unswept, uncleaned, and unventilated for one year! Will it not turn into a pigsty? Now think about what the soul of a man is like when he has not cleaned it through Confession, not only for a year, but for twenty, forty, sixty, or seventy years!...

4) A fourth man says: "I am confessing before God. What need is there for me to go to the priest?"

...God has ordained the priest to administer the Holy Sacraments so that we can receive through them heavenly all-saving grace. Confession is a sacrament, too. If you confess before God, you are doing well, because you are moving your conscience, remembering your sins, and maybe even shedding tears for them. Yet you do not receive God's grace of forgiveness through all that. As when you sit and think how, during the never-ending day of the Heavenly Kingdom, those who have pleased God partake of the unfathomable-for-us heavenly Communion, you do not partake in reality, no matter how moved you may be by your thought, until you accept visible Holy Communion; so too, until you go to the priest to whom Jesus Christ Himself has given the power to bind and loose, no matter how much you confess before God, you do not receive forgiveness for your sins, because God Himself has condescended to say to the priest: *whose soever sins ye remit, they are remitted unto them* (John 20:23).

Besides, Confession before a priest has an enormous instructive meaning. It humbles us. It cures our pride; it makes us blush savingly; it instills in us shame and fear and thus protects us from future sins. When we sin, we sin against the Omnipotent God, but we are not ashamed before Him because we do not see Him. In the same manner, when we confess before God, we do so easily, because we do not see Him, and it is as if we were talking to ourselves. But what shyness comes over us when we confess before the priests! The man who has submitted to the Church order to confess before a priest will hardly dare to repeat his sins, when he thinks of having to reveal them again during Confession.[2] Jesus Christ has ordered very wisely that our repentance should be done before a priest who is God's witness!

"But how can the priest absolve sins?" you ask. He can, since God has ordered it so. "But is the priest himself not a sinful man?" If he is sinful, what do you lose from that? He is sinful for himself and will answer before God for his sins. The Holy Sacraments administered by him do not cease to be active for you because of his sinfulness if you accept them with faith and humility. Does the sunray get dirty when it falls on mud? In the same way, God's grace does not lessen by being transmitted by a priest muddied with sins. He himself may be denied grace on Judgment Day because of his sinfulness, but you, accepting through him God's grace, will not deprive yourself of it if you show yourself to be worthy.

"But will the priest not give away the secret of my confessed sins?" No! No priest has the right to tell of that which he has heard during Confession. He has to take the secret of the Confession to his grave. So do not worry that the shame of your sinfulness may be announced to society.

But remember that if you avoid Confession because of zeal for your honor, you will shame yourself. If you are ashamed to admit your weaknesses before one man, everyone will begin

---

2. St. John Climacus, *The Ladder of Divine Ascent*, 7th edition (Sergiev Posad, 1908), p. 41.

talking about them! Such is the spiritual law. People sense our weaknesses, no matter how diligently we hide them. If you confess them before one man, God, because of your humility before this single witness, will cover you with His grace before the many.

However, if you are shielding your name before the confessor, your authority will collapse before all. Repent only before one man. Your confession will teach you to struggle with your passions; and if you are really fighting against them, the multitude of people will not find out about them. You, with God's help, will be healed before you have shamed yourself. But if you do not want to be healed through Confession, then you will both expose your name to abuse here and then be disgraced before the whole universe at the Last Judgment!

5) A fifth man says: "I am going to the priest to have him read the prayer of absolution for me."

This is the most sacrilegious abuse of Confession! What does "the prayer of absolution" mean? It means a prayer for the absolving of sins. The Christian goes to the priest and, without confessing his sins, asks him: "Father, say the prayer of absolution for me!" or "Forgiving prayer"; and the priest puts the stole on the head of the repenting man and forgives him the lawlessnesses which he has not confessed, but has hidden.

Stop, you, servant of God! What are you doing? Do you know what sins are hiding in this soul that you forgive them so carelessly? What a responsibility you carry before God, too! What if a deadly sin is being hidden from you, and you so thoughtlessly allow the Christian to partake of Holy Communion? Will you not speed up the death of his soul? Do you not know the words of the holy Apostle Paul: *Wherefore whosoever shall eat this bread, and drink this cup of the Lord, unworthily, shall be guilty of the body and blood of the Lord* (I Cor. 11:27). Why do you not test the believer? Why do you let him eat and drink his eternal condemnation? Why do you give the Sacrament to an unrepentant sinner? Judas, too, took Holy Communion together with the other holy Apostles at the Last Supper, but because he was an unrepentant sinner, instead of God's grace, Satan went into him. Do you want to make a second Judas out of the careless Christian who approaches Christ without Confession, only with an "absolving" prayer? It is better to refuse Holy Communion to the unprepared man until he repents and confesses than to give him fire and condemnation.

This reading of the prayer of absolution is the greatest misuse! It is both lying to God and lying to oneself. Ananias and Sapphira paid with their lives for their wicked attempt to deceive the Holy Spirit (cf. Acts 5:1-10). Do not fool yourself, Christian! The priest cannot forgive your sins until he hears them during Confession. He cannot loose the knots of your conscience until he has touched them. No prayer of absolution, lulling to your conscience, can help you. You have either confessed your sins and have received forgiveness for them, or you have not confessed them and they have stayed in your soul. If you can wash yourself without touching the water, then you will also be able to clean yourself from your lawlessness without confessing it.

The reading of the prayer of absolution, as a lulling of the conscience's vigilance, is a sin both for the priest and the layman, because in its core there is delusion and lies. This practice does not lead to spiritual healing, but to ever greater sinfulness. Someone is critically ill. The illness is identified with certainty, and the medicine which can overcome it is also precisely known; but because it is bitter, the sick man asks for something more pleasant. Then the doctor gives either morphine to dull the pain or some sweet but useless syrup. Will the sick man recover?

Never! And who will be responsible for his death? He himself, because he wanted sweet syrups to fool himself, and the doctor, who knew what he should give, but out of a desire to please the man did not give it.

Just recently a good and knowledgeable Christian woman confided in me the following: "I had prepared for Holy Communion. I went to church and looked for the parish priest so that I could confess. The priest was very busy, and his mood, as I noticed, was not good. He met me with a slight irritation: 'Well, why have you come? To confess all the same small sins? You do not have any big transgressions before God. Come here. I will read you the prayer of absolution!' 'But I want to confess; something is weighing me down!'—'There is no need! Come and kneel here!' I obeyed, and he read me the prayer of absolution. I got up and walked away, but there was no relief in my soul! The burden remained there and tormented me even more! I returned to the priest from the middle of the temple, but he was already busy with other worshipers. The time for Communion came. I did not dare to take Communion, because I did not feel that my conscience was cleared. On the next Sunday I went to another church. There I went to Confession and took Communion. I felt a great joy from the Confession; it was only then that I was relieved."

Editor's Note: The same warning may be said about the current practice of "general confession," that is, when the priest raises his epitrachelion to the whole congregation and recites the prayer of absolution for all, even though none have given a personal confession.

A priest prays for the welfare of his spiritual children.
Illustration from *Russian Pilgrim,* 1913.

V

Rules for a Saving Confession

ALL CHRISTIANS without exception must go to Confession if they wish to be saved. But how should the truly faithful Confession occur? Many do not know this, and that is why it is necessary to discuss this question more thoroughly. Here we will look at the following three parts of Confession:

a) What we should do before we go to the confessor.
b) What we should do when we are with the confessor.
c) What we should do when we come out of Confession.

What should we do before we go to the confessor?

The first and the last of the Apostles of Christ sinned gravely. Peter denied Christ; Judas betrayed Him. But Peter was forgiven and Judas perished. Peter regained his apostolic dignity, but the condemnation of the ages is still weighing on Judas. What saved Peter, and what destroyed Judas? What should have this wretch done? Should he have confessed the sin after he committed it? But, technically speaking, he confessed when he went to the scribes and the elders and told them, *I have sinned in that I have betrayed the innocent blood* (Matt. 27:4), and with the confession gave back the thirty silver pieces to them. Is this not enough? Alas, no! A confession by itself does not save. Besides a broken heart, a live faith in God's grace is needed. Judas despaired of his salvation; that is why he hung himself after his confession. His body hung on a tree, and his soul went to hell for eternal torment.

Peter did not do so. In the yard of Caiaphas he denied Christ, his Benefactor and Teacher, three times: *I do not know the Man* (Matt. 26:74). But at the third denial, when he heard the rooster crow, he remembered what Christ had prophesied, realized his sin, and humbled his heart. He went out of that yard, got out of the bad company of the servants of the high priest, and, most importantly, began to shed bitter tears—tears of sincere, heartfelt, deep repentance. According to one tradition, throughout his whole life, whenever he heard a rooster crow Peter remembered his heavy sin, and his eyes turned into two springs of most repentant tears. Peter did not despair; he believed in God's mercy and thus saved himself.

St. Peter has left us a living lesson: to turn again to God after our fall into sin. It is **faith in God's mercy** which drives away every despair. God is love. However grave our sin may be, He will forgive it, provided we repent from the heart. Even if our sins are as high as the mountains, they will sink in the ocean of God's mercy. However, if a man despairs, he is lost. Despair is the triumph of the devil. In short, let us protect ourselves from despair, because if we despair no one can save us.

We should imitate the holy Apostle Peter in another respect, as well. As he realized his sin, he immediately went out of the accursed yard of the high priest where he had denied Christ. And you, brother or sister, when you want to confess and come back to God, come out of that accursed yard of sin where you have been until now and where you have denied Christ not three times, but thirty-three times. Come out with your body, with your heart, and with your mind! Peter went away from the servants of the high priest. You, too, abandon the friendship with those who teach you to sin or who unwittingly serve as a temptation to you.

The most important moral from the behavior of the repentant Apostle is the following. When St. Peter was left alone, he reflected in himself, relived the horror of his sin, and **cried bitterly** because of deep suffering. As you prepare to go to your confessor, do not approach him without preparing beforehand. First go away from the noise of daily life, leave every other care, gather your thoughts, and make a short but heartfelt prayer. Remember all your sins and even write them down on a piece of paper, so that you will not forget them in your embarrassment, and thus remain uncleansed of them, when you go to Confession. Remember the ten commandments, see which one/s you have transgressed, recall whether you have committed a deadly sin, test your conscience, judge yourself, cry for your fall, and in such a mood go to the priest! Then you can be confident that you will receive true forgiveness, because *a heart that is broken and humbled, God will not despise* (Ps. 50:17).

Grieving over the sins committed by us is absolutely necessary, if we want to receive God's forgiveness. Indeed, this is what repentance consists of—to shed tears, to feel deep sorrow because of one's fall. As St. Isaac of Syria testifies, God accepts our repentant grief as an offering of repentance.[1]

This is what we need to do before we go to the confessor.

What should we do when we are with the confessor?

We have to do the following: 1) Remember that we have come to Christ's infirmary. Here, the visible doctor is the priest,

1. Protopriest G. Diatchenko, *Lessons and Examples of the Christian Faith*, (St. Petersburg), p. 547.

and the invisible—Christ Himself; 2) Confess our sins without false shame; 3) Not seek excuses for our sins; 4) Consciously conceal absolutely nothing; 5) Do not confess with general phrases which have no meaning; 6) Confess briefly, but precisely, the character of each of our sins; 7) Not reveal other people's sins, and conceal, whenever possible, the names of the persons who have tempted us or who have sinned with us through our fault; 8) Not to boast before the priest of any virtues of ours; 9) Not to transfer the blame on others, but only on ourselves; and 10) Have a sincere desire not to sin again.

1) When we go to Confession, **we enter Christ's infirmary.** Here God Himself is the Doctor, because only He can give and take away life, judge and acquit, punish and forgive. The priest is only a witness and a representative of God. That is why, standing visibly before the priest, and invisibly before Christ Himself, we must approach the great mystery of spiritual cleansing with great trembling! The priest hears our confession, but God accepts it. The priest examines our soul, but God will heal it. The priest will prescribe the remedies, but God will do the miracle of spiritual renewal.

Be heedful, Christian, to what infirmary you have come, so that you will not go away uncured because of carelessness or neglect, or ignorance or misplaced fear. If you truly have fear of God, be fearless when you come to confess your sins. The Judge before Whom you are standing is infinitely merciful! He is dreadful only for those who do not fear Him and in their thoughtlessness refuse to repent.

2) Your confession must be done **without false fear.** In this world, almost all of us live with a Pharisaic hypocrisy. We are one thing, but we want to pass for something else; we do not show ourselves outwardly as we are inwardly. We wish that

people would have a good opinion of us, and that is why we hide the bad qualities and show the good ones. If we do not have any good ones, we boast of imagined virtues. That is why you will often meet people in this life who seem to be good on the outside, but are not so in their hearts. Do we not lie to each other like that in this world? But should we lie when we are standing for Confession?

It is true that it is not easy to show yourself sinful before your confessor when you pretend to be good before everyone else. You feel ashamed to reveal your weaknesses. Yet how are you going to be cured if you hide your illness? You conquer your shame when you go to a doctor for examination—that is how you cure your body. Then why are you ashamed when you go to the priest to cure your soul? Do you not see that shame is an obstacle to your salvation? So shrug off the shame and get a grip on determination! You must be ashamed when you sin, not when you confess your sin! God has connected shame with sin, and determination with Confession. Do not listen to the devil who corrupts God's order and inspires shame at the confession of sin, but determination at its commission. He has turned everything upside down in order to destroy you.

When the famous Socrates was walking along a street in Athens, he saw one of his students who was coming out of the house of a certain harlot. The young man became ashamed in front of his teacher and quickly drew back inside again to hide. "Oh, young man," Socrates said to him, "it is not that shameful to come out of such a house, but it is shameful to remain in such a house." Oh, Christian, I will say, it is not that shameful to disclose your sin in Confession, but it is shameful to remain closed in it, that is, to conceal it from your priest. St. Basil the Great said: "The hidden sin is an incurable sickness of the soul."

How can you be cured from your illness if you hide it from the doctor?

Some are ashamed to confess because they have high posts and are high-ranking people, but look at the example of Bishop Potamius. He was of a respectable age, famous for his virtues, a model of celibacy. Yet it so happened that he fell in sin, but he got up immediately and thought of repenting at the council of all the bishops who were to meet soon in his town. When the council began, Bishop Potamius, being respected by all, was elected as chairman. He began to feel in his heart a horrendous struggle between shame and heartfelt repentance. "Potamius," shame was saying on one side, "are you really going to confess in public?"

"Potamius," repentance was calling on the other side, "why are you delaying and not doing that which you decided to do?"

"Are you not ashamed before the people?" reasoned shame.

"You be ashamed before God!" advised repentance.

"But you are a prelate! You will become a temptation!" reasoned shame.

"Precisely because of your being a prelate, you must give the world a good example!" cried repentance.

In the end repentance won, and shame retreated. Potamius got up from his chair and confessed his sin before all. Even the angels in heaven wondered at such a confession!

If a prelate was not ashamed to confess his sin before a whole council, why should we be ashamed to tell of our sins secretly before one servant of God? The moment we tell of them, they stop being sins. When David confessed his sins before Nathan, he immediately heard the comforting word, *The Lord has put away thy sin* (II Kings 12:13). But the unconfessed sin leaves an incurable, deadly wound on the soul. So let us confess boldly!

3) When we are standing before the court of voluntary confession, **we must not seek excuses for our sins.** Let us suffer in voluntary self-exposure. This suffering is expiatory. Let us blush with embarrassment. Our sins are burning in the flames of self-exposure. But if we begin to excuse ourselves, to justify ourselves, that is the end of the saving power of our confession. What is Confession?—repentance. And the truly repentant person knows only one thing—to cry and ask for mercy. If he begins to justify himself, to use cunning, all of his repentant mood will vanish into thin air. In the Sacrament of Confession the repentant mood is very important.

We must remember all of this, because there are many Christians who, as they confess, always want to excuse themselves in some way. Even though they confess their sin, they always try to make it less important and heavy, always looking for some extenuating circumstances, so that they will look more innocent. They must know that the heavenly court is not like the earthly one. Before the earthly court the defendant tries to make himself appear more innocent so that he will be acquitted. Before God's court it is the opposite: whoever accuses himself more is acquitted more.

Is it not for this that Jesus Christ is calling us to Himself, to forgive us all voluntary and involuntary sins? No other religion teaches of a God as full of love for men as ours does.

It is told about Blessed Jerome that, as he lived in Palestine and worked in the cave of Bethlehem where our Saviour was born, he had a wondrous vision on Christmas. Jesus Christ appeared to him as a child and asked him: "Jerome, when everyone presents something to me, what are you going to give me?"

"My virtues and prayers," answered St. Jerome.

"This is good, but what else?"

"My heart, my soul, and all of myself!"

"I accept that, too, but I want something else from you as well."

"But what else should I give You, Lord?" wondered the ascetic.

"Give me your sins!"

The Blessed Jerome began to cry brokenheartedly. He asked through tears: "Why do You need my sins, Lord?"

"I want to take them on myself!"

Do you hear? "Give me your sins!" Jesus Christ wants from us our sins. Let us give them to Him in the holy Sacrament of Confession, and He will forgive us for them.

4) **We must consciously hide absolutely nothing** before the priest. If we unwittingly forget a sin, we must confess it the next time. To conceal something for which our conscience is clearly bothering us would mean that we have doubled our sin: doubled, because one, we have committed it, and two, we have concealed it.

Do not hide your sin in your soul. It is a deadly disease. It is an ulcer which, if it is not operated on, can send you to the grave. By concealing our sins we are doing the greatest favor to the devil, who makes us commit lawlessness and afterwards keep it in our souls as his treasure, which will serve him as accusatory material against us. Confess everything which stains your conscience. The more waste you carry out of your soul of your own accord, the more your soul will be swept by God's grace. Whoever sins enters into an alliance with the devil, but whoever confesses breaks up his friendship with the demons. Confession is treason against the devil. It is the only virtuous treachery.

St. Bishop Ignatius Brianchaninov teaches us wonderfully: "Through the confession of sins the friendship with the demons is broken up. The hatred of sin is a proof of true repentance and of the determination of a man to lead a virtuous life. If you have adopted the habit of sinning, confess your sins more often, and soon you will free yourself from the captivity of sin. Lightly and joyously you will follow the Lord Jesus Christ. The friends of a man who constantly betrays them become his enemies and go away from him as from a traitor who continually seeks their certain peril; and the sins, too, draw back from the man who confesses them, because the sins are based and stand on the pride of the fallen nature and cannot stand exposure."[2]

5) In Confession **we must not use general terms** which do not mean anything. Many, especially among those confessing for the first time, learn what to say before the priest when they go to him. Either out of timidity or out of lack of experience, they often say inappropriate things and leave Confession without benefit.

A Christian woman decided to go to Confession, but she did not know what to do. She asked another woman for advice, and that woman taught her: "Say: 'I am guilty of everything!' and that is it." "Oh, it is very easy then," said the first Christian to herself and stood encouraged before the servant of God.

When the priest asked her about her sins, she calmly said: "Father, I am guilty of everything!" and thought that she had finished her confession. "And have you stolen any horses?" he unexpectedly asked. "Have I stolen horses?" she wondered. "It never occurred to me to commit such a sin!" "Ah, so you are not guilty of everything!" wisely said the priest. "There are people who do steal horses. But you, as it turns out, have not committed this sin. Let us see, one by one, in what you have sinned," so he led her to a true confession.

2. Bishop Ignatius Brianchaninov, *Works*, Vol. 3, (St. Petersburg, 1905), p. 102.

6) When we confess, we must tell **briefly and accurately** the nature of each of our sins. We see that general terms do not benefit the confessing person. He must recount individually each of his transgressions before God. Of course that does not mean that he must begin to tell long and detailed stories. The priest is usually a very busy man. During the feasts, and especially before Communion, many are waiting their turn to confess to him. That is why conciseness, accuracy, and briefness are needed. In order to achieve that, it is recommended that the sins be recorded beforehand on a piece of paper and that they be read during Confession. Do not wait for the priest to ask you questions. The benefit is much greater when you tell about your sins of your own accord. If the confessor stops you and, in order to clarify your spiritual condition for himself, asks you a question, you are obliged to answer accurately and straight to the point.

Some are cunning at Confession and, thinking that they can outwit even God, instead of briefly describing the nature of their sin—i.e., "I hate my neighbor"—out of an improper desire not to compromise themselves, begin to tell long and unnecessary stories of how their neighbor hated them, how he harmed them, etc. Again, instead of saying: "I stole such-and-such a thing," they begin explaining how someone else's property has been left with them. This is not a confession, but a foolish slyness before God.

7) During Confession, **we must not tell of other people's sins,** but only of ours, withholding whenever possible the names of the persons who have caused us to sin or whom we have tempted to sin with us.

Many do not abide by this natural rule and fall into the following unreasonableness: when they come to confess their sins, they speak only about those of other people: "She, my daughter-in-law, did this and that! My husband is an impossible boor!" or "My wife is not obeying me; she has a very bad character, and she is constantly quarreling with me and my family. A friend of mine, his name is so-and-so,—you know him, Father—has insulted me greatly. And so-and-so, Father did this!"

This is not Confession—to accuse others instead of yourself. Rather, it is a judgment of others. Those who do this come to the priest sinful and leave even more so!

8) Others, when they come to Confession, instead of exposing themselves, which is natural, necessary, and good during Confession, most unexpectedly begin **to boast**: "I, Father, have neither murdered nor stolen. Neither am I a drunkard. I live most respectably. I am held in respect by my neighbors and friends. Well, as a human, I might have sinned somehow at some time, but now I do not remember anything. My conscience is clear."

This terrible smugness is an even greater sin than those horrible sins which such a man boasts of never having committed, because he has sunk in the abyss of sin—dumb, complacent pride.

Many people arrive at the dulling of their moral sense and the belief that they are not sinful because of staying away too long from God's grace, which is given through the Sacraments of Christ's Church. The zealous servant of Christ from the village of Chepelare, the late Archpriest Eustathius Iankov, told me about one such man:

"My parishioner Bocho was a drunkard. He broke off with the Church and always hung around the bar. For a long time he did not come either to confess nor to take Communion. One evening his sister, who was a very devout Christian, called me.

"'Come, father, to confess and give Communion to Bocho. He is not sick, but since I know that he would not come to you, you go to him!'

"I went. I explained to him how good it would be for him to confess. But he stood silent. I asked him what was on his conscience. Was something bothering him?

"'There is nothing. My conscience is clear,' he said.

"'But how is it that there is nothing? Are you not a sinful man?'

"'I have done nothing wrong.'

"'And do you want to take Communion?'

"'Why not? I will take Communion,' he answered indifferently.

"'Good! Tomorrow I will come to your house with the Holy Gifts.'

"I went back home, but something was so heavy on my soul.

"Bocho's sister prepared him for Holy Communion—helped him to wash himself, gave him clean clothes to change into.

"On the next day I was carrying the Holy Gifts to Bocho's place. But I met some acquaintances of mine, and they told me: 'Bocho died unexpectedly last night!'

"I was numbed with horror. Obviously, God did not allow him to take Holy Communion, because he did not want to confess and be humbled before God by admitting to be sinful."

9) When we confess, **we must put the blame not on others, but on ourselves.**

In Paradise our ancestors Adam and Eve sinned: they ate from the tree with the forbidden fruit. God called them to confess, ready to forgive them: "Adam, where are you? Eve, what have you done?" Oh, if they **had confessed their sin bravely!** If they had admitted their guilt! If they had not transferred the blame each on the other! If Adam had said for himself, "God, forgive me! I am guilty!" and if Eve had hurried to admit: "No, Lord. Adam is not guilty, because I gave him to eat from the forbidden fruit!" If they had done so, they would not have been driven out of Paradise.

Instead, what did they do? When God spoke to them, they began to justify themselves and to transfer the blame one to the other. "Adam, what have you done?" "Not I, Lord, but the woman; she is to blame!" "Eve, what did you do?" "Not I, Lord; the snake, it tempted me." Both of them concealed their guilt. That is why they were driven out of Paradise.

But do not many among us do as Adam and Eve did? When we go to Confession, the priest asks: "Adam, in what condition are you? Eve, what have you done?" We justify ourselves, hide our sins, and blame others. This is not Confession! True Confession is a voluntary self-exposure before the confessor, fearless self-accusation, diligent self-compromise, virtuous self-shaming, deep brokenness, non-hypocritical sorrow for sins, and true desire for correction with God's help.

10) The crown of true repentance is the **firm intention not to sin any more in the future.**

There are people who confess only to be able to take Communion. They are led by the thought that the taking of Communion without Confession is a heavy sin for the soul, but they do not make the decision in their hearts to begin a new life. They think: "I will sin until the next Confession, and I will repent again; if there is Confession, the sin is not so frightful." And some even hurry to commit the sins which they desire but have not yet committed before they confess, so that they can report them in the coming Confession. All this is loathsome and base before God! Confession is not beneficial to the one who consciously follows the sinful whimsies of his perverted will and transgresses God's commands on purpose. Such a man who creates sinful habits in himself later wonders in vain why, when he confesses, he cannot correct himself! He cannot correct himself because he himself does not want to.

St. Basil the Great says: "It is not he who says: 'I have sinned,' but after that continues to sin that is confessing his sin, but it is he who, according to the words of the Psalm, has seen his sin and has hated it. Of what use is the care of the doctor to the sick man when the one suffering from the diseases is holding steadfastly to that which is detrimental to life? In the same way, there is no use in forgiving the injustices of the man who continues to commit them. The one who continues to live in debauchery does not benefit from the loosing of the sin of debauchery. The wisest Home-builder of our life wants the one who has lived in sins and afterwards has given a vow to begin a new life, to put an end to his past and, after the committed sins, lay a beginning as a person ready for a new life through repentance."[3]

In order for us to have true benefit from Confession, we must firmly resolve not to sin any more in the future. True repentance, according to the Holy Fathers, is in exactly this, not to repeat your sin any more! "Whoever allows himself to sin arbitrarily, with the hope that he will repent," says St. Isaac the Syrian, "deals treacherously with God. Death strikes him unex-

3. Protopriest Diatchenko, *op. cit.*, p. 556.

pectedly, and he does not live to the time which he presumed to devote to virtue."[4]

In order for us to have true benefit from Confession, we must resolve not to sin in the future. True repentance, according to the Holy Fathers, consists precisely in not repeating the sin any more. In order for this to happen, in Confession we must wish with all our heart to begin a new life in the future. If we have this saving desire, let us be confident that God will help us by all means.

What Should We Do When We Leave the Confessor?

After we have confessed well, we must carry out the penance which has been given to us: bows, intensified prayer, fasting, diligent reading of God's Word, almsgiving, visiting the sick, caring for orphans, etc. We must pay special attention to the following three points:

1) If you have an enmity against someone, **forgive with all your heart**, so that God will also forgive you (cf. Matt. 6:14-15). Otherwise, your confession will be in vain.

Themistocles and Aristides, distinguished Athenian governors, were in constant enmity between themselves. But their country assigned them to do an important state job together. However, how could they abandon the enmity? Then Aristides said: "Themistocles, do you want to leave the enmity here, on the border? We will go, do the job, and, if you want, when we come back, we will renew our enmity!"—and so they did. After successfully completing the state job, they came back and again continued to be hostile to each other.

4. Ibid, p. 556.

Does it not happen so with Christians who are on hostile terms? They confess, take Communion from the same cup, and leave the hostility on the threshold of the temple; but when they leave the church, they renew the enmity again.... Is this Confession? They are committing a greater sin by confessing and taking Communion without wanting to give up hatred towards their personal enemies. Let us put an end to enmities!

2) Others who have admitted in Confession that they have violated their celibacy or family honor must **give up the bad road forever**. They cannot love both the sin and God.

A philosopher once went boating in the sea. There was a strong storm which almost overturned his boat. It was a miracle that he survived. He came back home and, since one of his windows was overlooking the sea, immediately walled up that window, so that he would not look towards the sea and fall into the temptation of wanting to go boating again!

Oh, Christian, how many times you, too, have almost lost both your life and your soul in the sea of lewd love! You have been delivered by a miracle. Now avoid the causes for it! Do not go by that road anymore. Do not enter that house anymore. Do not look toward that window anymore. Close your eyes so that the temptation will not enter your heart. Otherwise, you will perish!

3) Finally, if you have misappropriated another's possession, if you have robbed someone, **return that which does not belong to you.** Otherwise, there is no forgiveness for you.

If you blaspheme God's name, if you deny Orthodoxy, if you are angry, if you are proud, if you envy, or commit other heavy sins—when you repent, everything will be forgiven you. Why? Because with all of these sins you offend God, and God has made the priest His representative for all these sins with which men offend Him. As God's representative, the priest can forgive you the sins against God if you repent.

However, if you keep another's property and confess it but do not return it, the priest does not have the right to forgive you. If you are holding in your hands the property of some poor man, how can the priest forgive you for this sin? The poor man has not made the priest his substitute and has not given him the power to forgive his stolen property on his behalf.

But you will say: "I give alms to the monasteries and the poor!" Be quiet! No law, either of God or of man, allows anyone to give away as a gift to someone another man's property. Therefore, in order to receive forgiveness from God, return that which does not belong to you!

We see then what the rules are for a saving Confession: first, before we go to the confessor, we must examine well our conscience; second, when we are with the priest, we must confess sincerely, with a broken heart, and without shame and excuses; third, when we leave the priest, we must carry out our penance, put an end to the hostility, give up our impure life, and return that which is not ours.

He who does not correct his behavior through Confession does not confess but talks idly, according to the words of St. Basil the Great.[5]

5. Ibid, p. 540.

"REPENTANT IMPRESSIONS OF GREAT LENT"
A painting by E. Alexandrovsky. From *Russian Pilgrim*, no. 13, 1902.

VI

Consequences of True Confession

ABBA ISAIAH reasons: "Let us fulfill that which is necessary according to our strength, and the great might of our Lord Jesus Christ will help us.... He knows that man is wretched, and that is why He has presented him with repentance throughout the entire time of his earthly life. Mighty and saving repentance acts over us until our last breath."[1]

Wondrous are the consequences of true Confession! "The truly repentant man receives forgiveness for his sins, is reconciled with God, the Church, and his own conscience, and thus regains the precious filial striving towards God as his Father, and benefits from all the gifts of His fatherly love and kindness."[2]

The consequences of true Confession reflect not only on the soul of the repenting person, they make a reflection on heaven also. There is great joy there over the repentant sinner (cf. Luke 15:10). The angels are rejoicing, the saints are cheered, and God Himself is glad, because a lost sheep has been found; God's drachma is found, on which the regal image of God is printed.

---

1. *Otechnik* by St. Ignatius Brianchaninov (St. Petersburg, 1880), p. 192.
2. Diatchenko, p. 540.

Through Confession all sins are erased, and the mark of righteousness is given to the sinner who has repented.

It was reported to a righteous bishop about two women that they did not live in celibacy. He turned to God with the request to reveal to him the truth about them. His wish was to help them in their salvation, and God heard his prayer.

After a Divine Liturgy, when the believers began to approach the Holy Sacraments to receive Communion, the bishop's spiritual eyes were opened under the influence of God's grace. He began to see the people's souls through their faces. Some were black and ugly, and others, bright and beautiful. When those two women who had immoral behavior approached the Holy Cup, the bishop saw that they had bright faces and beautiful, white clothes. When they took Communion, they began to shine even brighter. The bishop wondered what that meant and in his wonder turned to God for an explanation. Immediately, an angel of the Lord appeared. To the question of the bishop whether the report against these two women was rightful, the angel answered affirmatively.

"But then, how did they appear before the Holy Sacraments with bright faces, and how did they become even brighter afterwards?" asked the bishop.

The angel said: "You are amazed at that? You are right to be amazed, because you are human, but our Bishop and yours is God, man-loving and kind in nature. He not only does not send to the torment those who give up their sins and turn to Him with Confession, but He also puts an end to His anger towards them and favors them with honors. *For God so loved the world that He gave His Only-begotten Son* for it (John 3:16). If the Son of God has deigned to die for His enemies, would He not even more give forgiveness of sins and eternal delight to those who have become His own children and are repentant of

The first Communion of the Disciples of Christ
at the Mystical (Last) Supper, and the Communion
of the faithful of the Church.

their sins? Know with certainty that not one human sin can defeat God's love for man if only he washes away with repentance the evil which he has done before. Having love for man, God knows the feebleness of your race and the power of the passions and the devil's cunningness. That is why, when people fall into sin, God endures long, waiting for them to repent. And toward those who confess and toward those who beg for His grace, He shows compassion as toward feeble people and immediately sets them free from their punishment and presents them with the blessings prepared for the righteous."[3]

Many are the examples which convince us that all sinners who confess their sins with a sincere and deep repentance receive full pardon and salvation from God.

St. Niphont had the beneficial gift of seeing the spiritual world as clearly and well as we see physical objects. One day he went to church to pray. There the heavens above him opened, the roof of the temple disappeared, and he saw a road which led from the earth to the heavens. On this road angels were carrying the soul of a deceased man, and the demons crowded behind them, calling:

"Why are you taking this soul away from us? Or do you not know that, while living on earth, he was guilty of lewdness, robbery, and avarice? He is guilty of all kinds of sins!"

"We know!" answered the angels. "We know that this soul is very sinful, but we also know that he cried a lot for his sins and, before his death, confessed them. That is why the merciful and compassionate Lord forgave him all sins."

"But if even this soul has received pardon from God," yelled the demons, "then take to yourselves all sinners. Why are we laboring then?"

"Remember," answered the angels, "that all sinners who confess their sins with a broken heart receive pardon from God. But whoever dies without repenting, him God will condemn to eternal torment with you!"[4]

The distinguished Russian writer of spiritual books, St. Ignatius Brianchaninov, tells of the following event concerning the power and consequences of true Confession:

---

3. *Ancient Paterikon,* 2nd edition (Moscow, 1891), p. 364.
4. Lives of the Saints (of St. Dimitry of Rostov), Nov. 23.

"In the area of Vologda, Russia, there is a big village—Kubenskoe, which has several parishes. One of the parish priests fell ill, and, approaching his end, he saw his bed surrounded by demons who were getting ready to seize his soul and snatch it to hell. Then three angels appeared. One of them stood by the bed and began to argue for his soul with the most repulsive of the demons, who was holding an open book where all the sins of the priest were recorded.

In the meantime, the other parish priest came to confess and give Communion to his fellow-priest. The Confession began. The ill man, directing his frightened eyes towards the demons' book, told of his sins with self-denial, as if he were casting them out of himself. And what did he see? He saw clearly that when he told of some sin, this sin disappeared from the book: the writing was erased and only a blank spot was left. In this way, through his Confession, he erased all of his sins from the demons' book and was healed quickly.

He spent the rest of his days in deep repentance, and for their edification he told his neighbors about his vision, the proof of which was his miraculous healing.[5]

Some, reading these examples, will shake their heads distrustfully and say: "This is wonderful, but it is only a story in a book. Why can't I feel the regenerating power of Confession at least once in my life? I have confessed more than once, but I see that I am still the same. I am even becoming worse. Why do I not have such gracious experiences which convince me of the benefit of the Sacrament of Confession?"

The best answer to this question we find in the following account by the Holy Fathers: "Two monks went to the great Elder, Abba Zinon. Each of them confessed their sins privately.

---

5. Bishop Ignatius Brianchaninov, *Works,* Vol. 2, (St. Petersburg, 1905), p. 697.

Not long after that, a conversation was begun between the two monks. One of them asked:

"When we were with the Elder for Confession, did you benefit from it?"

"Yes," answered the other, "God healed me by his prayers."

"But I," complained the first one, "even though I confessed, did not feel relief."

The second one asked, "How did you confess before the Elder?"

The first one answered, "I told him: 'Abba, pray for me. Such-and-such thoughts are disturbing me.'"

"And I," said the second, "when I was confessing my sins to him, bathed his feet with my tears, and because of his prayers God healed me."[6]

Those who confess without feeling, coolly and formally, do not receive benefit from the Confession. Superficial, cold, and slack confession does not save. Humility, brokenness of heart, tears, and deep regret for our having been friends with the demons and in enmity toward God, are needed.

When the Prophet David committed a serious offense before God, he looked for a sacrifice worthy for the atonement for his great sin; and he did not find a better sacrifice than humility and a broken and repentant heart (Ps. 50:19). If we, too, humble our hearts and confess sincerely, we cannot but feel the wondrous results of repentance, the most tangible of which is the sweet peace of the conscience and the deep, renewed love for God which makes the heart shine with happiness.

---

6. Ibid.

VII

Closing Questions

SOME ASK: to what priest can a man confess? The answer is: to anyone who is Orthodox and has received the grace for performing the Holy Sacraments through a lawful ordination. He can be either young or old. Of course, it is recommended to find an experienced man who, because of his many years or his personal authority, can influence the confessing person more beneficially. However, if such a man cannot be found, we must not deprive ourselves of the spiritual benefits brought about by Confession for that reason only. Grace is active in the young priest with the same strength that it is in the old one.

Others ask, when should we confess?

Some answer hastily: during Great Lent; that is the time for Confession. But is this the right solution to the question? If someone falls seriously ill and asks your advice about when to call the doctor, will you tell him, "Wait for Great Lent?!" No, you will call the doctor immediately. If you care for the body in this way, you should care for the soul even more.

It is best not to postpone Confession at all. If today a ray of God has penetrated the room of your soul and has shown you with its appearance how much dust is flying there in the air and how much litter lies in the corners, do not postpone the

Death comes to an unrepentant sinner.
A 19th-century engraving from the book, *Spiritual Instructions to the Penitent.*

Confession with which you can clean your spiritual home. If today a divine word has moved your heart and has made you loathe your impurity, immediately wash yourself in the bath of repentance. If today God has knocked on your conscience, hurry to your priest and be reconciled with your Lord. Do not put it off for the next day. Who knows what unexpected thoughts will come over you tomorrow? Will you have the same repentant mood after today? God has promised to forgive you if you repent today, but He has not promised anywhere that you will live until tomorrow. On the contrary, He tells you that you do not know either the day or the hour of your death. So confess immediately when you feel the necessity. There are people who say: "I will repent in my old age." But do they realize how

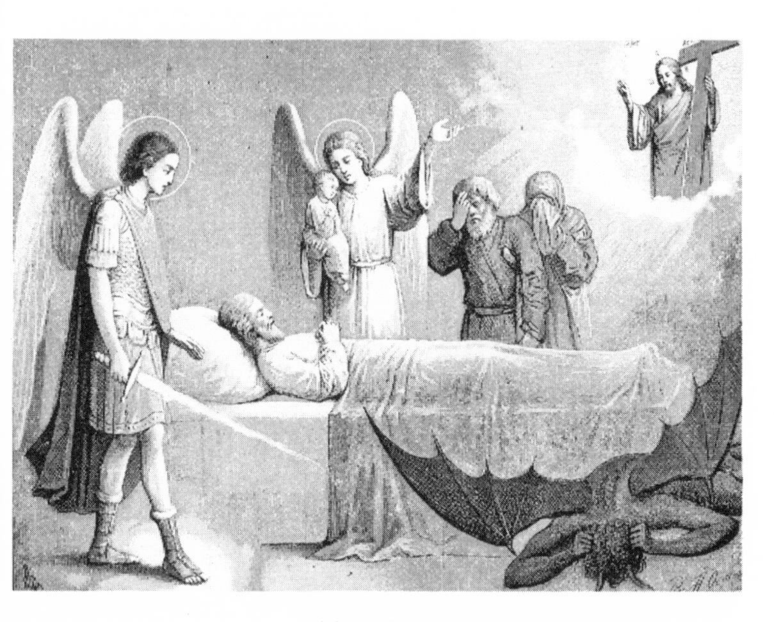

A blessed repose.
A 19th-century engraving from the book, *Spiritual Instructions to the Penitent.*

unreliable the support is that they are leaning on? Some people leave this life relatively young, and many are those who have been called to the other side suddenly. The Psalmist, seeing the human fates from the height of heaven, speaks about people that they all *go down to the dust,.. and none can keep alive his own soul* (cf. Ps. 21:30). If we cannot keep ourselves alive, however passionately we may be clutching life, we must take care to be reconciled with God in Confession while we have time, because *it is a fearful thing to fall into the hands of the living God* (Heb. 10:31).

Do not give in, brother, to the suggestions of friends who tell you comfortingly: "Wait to confess until you get ill, then the priest will come to confess you and give you Holy Communion." You should answer: "Many times the priest is called to the sick man only when his tongue is tied, and the conscience is dimmed. Then it is too late; then the sick man cannot confess even if he wants to. And if the same happens to me? If my tongue is paralyzed? If a senile sclerosis of the brain or some other disease takes away my memory? Then I cannot remember and confess my sins. Then none of my friends can help me. That is why I will confess now, while I am strong and remember all!"

Such a decision is saving. And so, do not postpone your Confession!

Of course, there are occasions for repentance and Confession which are more specifically established by the Holy Church. These are the four fasts of the year, when the Christian is obliged to fast and to prepare to take Holy Communion. If it is recommended to approach the holy Sacrament of Confession every time it is needed, this is even more pressing before the taking of Holy Communion.

What is Holy Communion?—The receiving of our Saviour and Lord in our heart. When we are expecting a high guest, we clean the rooms and change the air; we put them in order, and then we invite the guest with joy. How much more carefully should we prepare our souls when we are about to welcome the greatest Guest from heaven—Jesus Christ! Whoever confesses before Communion is inviting the Lord into a quiet, pleasant, and joyful corner of his heart. But whoever does not confess before Communion is inviting the heavenly Guest into the dirty and uncleaned room of his soul to insult Him. With that disregard towards his high Guest, he is driving Him away, and then the demons come and settle among the cobwebs and the litter.

Holy Communion is a two-edged sword. It sanctifies and burns; it justifies and condemns; it gives life and puts to death. Only those who have confessed beforehand benefit from it.

Those who approach it carelessly are greatly harmed. They eat and drink their own condemnation. Some of them, according to the words of the holy Apostle Paul, fall into various infirmities and diseases, and others die suddenly to go into eternal torment. All of this happens because they have not tested themselves beforehand, that is, they have not confessed (cf. I Cor. 11:27-31).

Is Holy Communion to be blamed for this? It is not to be blamed, but our negligence and carelessness are. Give the best dishes to a sick stomach, and they will upset it even more. Here, it is not the dishes which are to be blamed, but it is the one who eats them before he has been healed.

If someone has a wound and puts ointment on it before he has cleaned and disinfected it, he will inflame it even more. In the same manner, the man who does not confess before Communion compounds his sin. Confession cleans the sinful wound of the soul, and Holy Communion puts ointment on the wound. The wise Christian, listening to the call of the holy Church: "Come forth with fear of God, with faith, and with love!", does not dare to boldly show his faith in Holy Communion and his love for Christ before he has been filled with the saving fear of God and has realized it in the holy Sacrament of Confession.

The end goal of Confession is for the soul to be thoroughly cleaned, to be adorned and dressed up as a bride, so that it can meet worthily its heavenly Bridegroom, for Whom it was created. A soul which confesses regularly is like a house which is constantly swept. Conscience always stands as a watchful guard in front of such a clean house in order not to let in anything which should not be inside. If the unclean spirit who has come out of there becomes envious of the virtuous purity of such a renewed soul and wants to come into it again—seeing it empty,

swept, and put in order (cf. Matt. 12:44)—the conscience does not let it inside anymore. It repels everything which is foreign, base, loathsome, and sinful, and then Jesus Christ Himself comes and knocks on the door. *Behold, I stand at the door and knock: If any man hear My voice, and open the door, I will come in to him* (Rev. 3:20). *If a man love Me, he will keep My words: and My Father will love him, and We will come unto him and make our abode with him* (John 14:23).

The vigilant conscience of the man who confesses constantly hears the knocking of Christ, opens the door, and says: *Come, Lord Jesus!* (Rev. 22:20). "For it is You that my soul is longing for! It is You Whom it has waited for for so long! Come and abide in me...." And the Divine Guest comes into such a soul and stays to abide there eternally.

Blessed are they whose iniquities are forgiven, and whose sins are covered (Ps. 31:1). The barrier between him and God has fallen, and he is in full, blissful, and eternal union with his Lord! Amen!

Index